The Let's Talk Library™

Let's Talk About Staying in a Shelter

Elizabeth Weitzman

The Rosen Publishing Group's
PowerKids Press™
New York

For everyone—especially the kids—at the Jennie Clarke Residence.

Published in 1996 by The Rosen Publishing Group, Inc.
29 East 21st Street, New York, NY 10010

First Edition

Book design: Erin McKenna

Photo credits: Cover and pp. 4, 11, 12, 16, 19 by Sarah Freidman; p. 7 © Vision Impact Photo/International Stock; p. 8 © Ryan Williams/International Stock; p. 15 © Scott Thode/International Stock; p. 20 © Rae Russel/International Stock.

Weitzman, Elizabeth.
    Let's talk about staying in a shelter/ Elizabeth Weitzman.
    p.   cm. — (The let's talk library)
    Includes index.
    Summary: Briefly describes various kinds of shelters for people without permanent homes and discusses how to deal with living in one.
    ISBN 0-8239-2311-8
    1. Shelters for the homeless—United States—Juvenile literature. 2. Homeless children—United States—Juvenile literature. [1. Shelter for the homeless. 2. Homeless persons.] I. Title. II. Series.
    HV4505.W38 1996
    363.5'8—dc20   95-26713
                                                                                            CIP
                                                                                             AC

Manufactured in the United States of America

Table of Contents

Mañuel

On a cold January morning, seven-year-old Mañuel stood at the front door of a tall brick building. His mother held one of his hands. In the other he clutched a big plastic bag filled with all his clothes and toys. Even though he was cold, Mañuel didn't want to go inside.

Mañuel and his mother are homeless. A flood destroyed their apartment. They were sent to a place called a **shelter** (SHELL-ter). Mañuel was scared. He didn't know what to expect.

◀ New situations can be scary.

What Is a Shelter?

A shelter is a place where people can go when they don't have a home. Thousands of kids stay in shelters every year.

Going somewhere new is always hard, whether it's to a new school, a new city, or a new building. Sometimes you have to go to all three at once. There will be lots of changes when you go to a shelter. One thing will always stay the same: Every shelter has other kids who feel just like you do.

You may make new friends at a shelter. ▶

One-Room Shelters

There are different kinds of shelters. Sometimes people stay in shelters where everybody sleeps and eats in one big room. Most people only stay in these one-room shelters for a little while.

Because there are so many people, you'll see some unusual things. You might see people crying or fighting. It's normal to be scared when you see things like that. As long as you stay with your family, you'll be safe.

◀ It can be hard to live in a place where you have no privacy.

Hotels

Some families who have lost their homes stay in a hotel shelter. People usually stay in hotels for several months.

In a hotel, your family will have its own room. You'll probably share a kitchen and bathroom.

It's hard to share a small space with so many people. So try hard to **respect** (ree-SPEKT) your family, and ask them to respect you.

You may have to learn to share space in a bathroom if you live in a hotel. ▶

Residences

Most families go to **residence** (REH-zi-dents) shelters after they've stayed in a hotel for a while. At these shelters, each family has its own apartment.

Most hotels and residences have a special room just for kids, with tutors for homework and fun activities. It's not a good idea to hang out in the hallways or stairwells, but the kids' room is usually a great place to spend time and make new friends.

◀ You'll find other kids to play with in the kids' room.

Rules

Because there are so many people living in shelters, there are lots of rules. But the most important rule never changes: Respect other people. If you don't want other people to use your toys or play loud music at night, don't do it yourself.

Never fight with people who don't follow the rules. They probably won't change, and you could get hurt. If people don't have respect for you, stay away from them.

You, and everyone else, must follow the rules in the ▶ shelter, such as waiting for your turn in line for food.

What Can You Do to Help?

Your dad might seem angry or sad since you've moved to a shelter. That makes sense. He has to think about finding a new home and keeping you safe and happy.

That's a lot to worry about. But you can help. If your dad needs some time alone, take your little sister to the kids' room to play. This will help your dad, and it'll help you. If your dad is more relaxed, he'll be able to give you the attention you deserve.

◀ You can help your dad have one less thing to worry about by watching out for your younger sister.

Your Feelings

It's important to take care of yourself too. Every kid who stays in a shelter gets scared sometimes. At new places there are always strange smells and odd noises.

You may be **embarrassed** (em-BAYR-est) or angry about living in a shelter. Or you could be worried about where you're going next. You may be sad without knowing why. There's only one thing to do when you're upset: Talk about how you're feeling.

Everyone who stays in a shelter gets scared or sad sometimes. ▶

Talk About It!

There's nothing wrong with any of your feelings. But if you keep them hidden, you'll only feel worse.

Talk to your mom or dad about how you are feeling. If you don't feel comfortable doing that, talk to a teacher or an adult at the shelter. Once you tell someone how you feel, that person can help you understand your feelings.

◀ Talking to your mom about how you're feeling can help you feel better.

Home Is Where Your Heart Is

The most important thing about a home isn't something you can touch or hold. It's not a TV or a stereo or even a house. It's love.

There is always someone for you to love. It may be your dad, your mom, your grandma, your best friend, or your brother. It might even be a minister or counselor. No matter how hard things are right now, don't forget that as long as you have—and give—love, you'll be okay.

Glossary

embarrassed (em-BAYR-est) Feeling ashamed or uncomfortable.

residence (REH-zi-dents) A place to live.

respect (ree-SPEKT) To be considerate of someone.

shelter (SHELL-ter) A place where people can go when they've lost their home.

Index